Fatima is from the United Arab Emirates, she worked hard in her medical field and wanted to make her mark in writing and poetry. Fatima has read other writers in various fields and has been affected by people's social aspects – all that influenced her to write. Also, she was touched by her dear mother who was a good reader. All that refined her love for writing and encouraged the author to put together her writings to present a book in your hands.

To anyone who likes to read different English poetry.

Fatima

SEARCHING FOR LIGHTS

Illustrations by
Hessa Alneaimi

AUSTIN MACAULEY PUBLISHERS™
LONDON • CAMBRIDGE • NEW YORK • SHARJAH

Copyright © Fatima 2024
Illustrations by: Hessa Alneaimi

The right of Fatima and Hessa Alneaimi to be identified as author and illustrator of this work has been asserted by them in accordance with Federal Law No. (7) of UAE, Year 2002, Concerning Copyrights and Neighboring Rights.

All rights reserved. No part of this publication may be reproduced, stored in a retrieval system, or transmitted in any form or by any means, electronic, mechanical, photocopying, recording, or otherwise, without the prior permission of the publishers.

Any person who commits any unauthorized act in relation to this publication may be liable to legal prosecution and civil claims for damages.

The age group that matches the content of the books has been classified according to the age classification system issued by the Ministry of Culture and Youth.

ISBN – 9789948779940 – (Paperback)
ISBN – 9789948779957 – (E-Book)

Application Number: MC-10-01-0590631
Age Classification: E

Printer Name: iPrint Global Ltd
Printer Address: Witchford, England

First Published 2024
AUSTIN MACAULEY PUBLISHERS FZE
Sharjah Publishing City
P.O Box [519201]
Sharjah, UAE
www.austinmacauley.ae
+971 655 95 202

I would like to acknowledge and give my thanks to Austin McCauley Publishers for their efforts and cooperation. So thank you for encouraging this book and thank you for choosing me as a writer among you; without your support this work could not have been done.
Sincerely, thank you.

To every one reading my book, I appreciate your time and thank you lots.

Ruqayya Khaled and Aliya Khaled: your support and encouragement meant a lot to me.
Thank you.

Special thanks to: Hessa Alneaimi
What is bigger than thank you to write to you?
You drew my dream, and you were a life ring when I got lost with my book.
The cover and the drawings by: Hessa Alneaimi
Some drawings were done by the writer

Last line:
My Husband Mohammed *"Just tell me"* How I can thank you enough.

Fatima

Shadows

A gap in your life after me
You dragged yourself in that hollow
You will be lost in the dark
Between the 'shadows'
Your new fellows
You will get scared
You will never find the light
And you will never find 'me' again.

It's Ticking

Its ticking, oh I can feel it
Ticking!
Taking me back
To that paused promise
Subconsciously
Time is over
And the hour is ticking
Declaring
That jammed memory is alive again
I can't take you out of my head
And I love you again
Myself is deceiving me

Internal clock disturbing
Indicating suffering
I was free for some years
But I am back to your prison
To that promise,
To search for you
And love you again
It's loud
No stop
No snooze
It's getting louder
And I love you more
When is salvation
I can't escape
It's my brain! Betraying me
Won't turn it off
Who can rescue me?
I am falling
Drowning in that pool of memories
Killing me
I am tired
Scared to go back and too drained this way
Damaged in both sides
Oh, how…
How can I stop it?
How can I go on like this?
I am a total mess
Caught
In my own trap.

*****

Sometimes

Sometimes we call the past…
We relive it again
Walking forward in a backward way
Lost eyes
Shook heart
Its
Empty soul
Guilty soul

We give our back to who cared

Digging the past searching for people who gave us their back…
Loved them
Missed them
Its
Empty soul
Guilty soul

When rainbows turn grey
Where the beauty wears black
No flowers rich in color
Its
Empty soul
Guilty soul

Sometimes when the past rises…
Darkness rises and the light cries
We close our eyes
Intentionally
Its
Empty soul
Guilty soul

Sometimes. We kill the soul
Dead soul living the past…
Giving its back to who cared
Its
Empty soul
Guilty soul.

*****

Mirror

Hey…
You
In the glass
Me

***

Take me there
To your reversed world
and
Reverse everything

***

Reverse the pain
The tears
The guilt
And the darkness

***

You know my flaws
You witnessed my tears
You listened and never blamed me
You were a good reflection to me

***

But you can't reach out to me
You are a prisoner in a glass
A stronger version of me, though
Watching the story of my life silently

***

Who can help it!
Who?
You… Me?

Reflect some love
Some hope
I am waiting for the sparks
I am searching for lights
Maybe
Just one light.

***

It's Ended

It's ended, the dream is ended… I wake up and now…
I am just a Stranger in your Heart…

Pinkish days are ended… And I realized that they were, just white days and black nights…
And I am just a stranger in your heart…

I loved the fake and I built castles with no base…
I refused the fact…
I am Just a Stranger in your Heart.

You Left

You left and kept the wound opened
Bleeding memories
Confused thinking
Soured heart
Scary questions of your coming back

How could you think of this ending?
Unbelievable disappearance
Crazy planned escape
You left a heart
With a dead hope of your coming back

I never thought you could do it
The love you claimed
The dreams you dreamed
The fights we played
And your sweet ways of your coming back

The wound is still bleeding
The memories are suffocating
You left and I am still confused
Was the healing a goodbye
Or the healing was your coming back.

*****

I Left

It was the time to leave
I left and it was hard
I left and that was wise
I stabbed the promises
I crushed the dreams
For you not for me

I resist coming back
I tried, I wanted
But I closed my heart

I stopped thinking
I paused the feeling
For you not for me

I still remember your voice
Music playing with my thoughts
Calling me
I still remember your deep eyes
And how much I drown in them
I was feeling you were calling me
But I couldn't go back
For you not for me

I missed you and I was not selfish
I gave you a space
I wrote poems for you
I played back the memories
I wanted to go back
But I didn't
I couldn't
For you not for me

There was too much more
Too much pain and restless nights
Too much tears and no understanding
Too much differences and sweet illusions
And there was no one single hope
For you and for me.

*****

Without You

It's like the sunset all the day without you
When the birds stop singing
When the flowers close their petals
When all go home
And my home is not a home
I set and look at
Your empty chair
Imagining you reading a book
Or chatting on the phone

Those books were abandoned
And the phone stopped ringing
Frozen life in that home
I could hear your voice sometimes
Recorded between those sad walls
Holding them up
And
Sensing your soul walking around
Holding me up
Remembering you laugh makes me cry
Missing you is really harsh
Everything is missing
Everything is strange
It's like I was injured but still in pain
It's like I was broken but still cracked
I lost my treasure
The joy… the shine of life
It's like the sunset lasting all day
It's just like the sun said good bye forever
Without you.

******

The River Drop

She was a river's drop that loved the moon
Whenever he shows up, night or before noon
She jumps, just to reach the nearest tree's leaf
To see the moon… to stare at him… with loving eyes… with a shaky heart…

Sometimes the moon feels… and it's so harsh, so cruel because
He knows
He is the loved one
He is the wanted one
He is the one…
One day, before sunrise, after tiredness and rest, after hopelessness and hope
The white moon rose
So, with all the love and missing feelings she got
The transparent drop rose and called
My moon… my moon… my moon
And by the power he got, carelessly and proudly he called
My 'sun' star… my 'sun' star… my 'sun' star
With a disappointed eye… she froze
With a broken heart… she cried
Freezing and crying she was, and all of her, drowning in tears
Remembered
I am just a river's drop
And he is the Moon.

With a painful voice
The river was calling
Come back my softest drop
Come back my purest drop
Come back before the sunrise comes back

But because she loved the mighty and she is so little…
And because she remembered that… she is a river's drop
and he is the moon…
She 'froze'!

And the river still calling
Still crying…
Come back my baby drop…
Come back my purest baby drop…
Come back before the sun rises come back…
She froze, didn't want to move… couldn't move…

With all the power she got…
'Sun' rose…

And
Because she froze
Didn't want to move…

She 'vanished'!

The river's drop vanished… evaporated and ended.…
And chose the end of her story… and the hopeless love she lived… Suicide by the fire of her moon's sun…

*****

Fog

You don't love her
It's just a crush
And she will crush you up
Don't love her

She will dump you
She doesn't love you
Don't be dumb

Wash up the fog on your eyes
Watch me standing there

Her silky soft talk
Is pulling you to her web
Pull yourself together
Before you regret it
And regret losing me in the fog.

****

HE

Someone I created in my mind
I chose his name
His shape
His voice
His way
And He was
Just a name

*

I wrote a story
A Love novel
In my head!
He was my hero and I was his princess
I put the rules
And he had a role
It was everything
And He was
Just a love story

*

I was living my fantasy
Happy with the events I created
The imagination I imagined
The character I invented
He was mine
My dream
He was
Just a dream
And just a dream!

*

God!
I saw him
Handsome charming
He was real
No.!
But yes!
My dream became true
I followed him
The shape the voice the character
He was my Dream in Person!
What a gift
Just a gift

*

But who was she
He was holding her hand
Walking proudly with her
Crushing me

When I saw my dream with someone else
That wasn't in my novel
Who wrote this ending?
Not my pen
Not my heart!

I created everything in you
But
I couldn't write your heart
I wished you didn't appear
And stayed there hidden
Patting my thoughts
Like a breeze gently caressing my heart

This life was deforming the beauty

Who stabbed me now?
Life?

My pen or myself?
I am 'really' injured
And
He should have remained
Just a dream.

Good Morning Sun

Good morning sun
Set please
Hurry up
I want to meet him
At night
Mid of the night
Everybody sleeps

No one knows
Our secret!
Our own world
Our souls meet
In a 'dream'

*

And here we are
We laugh… We talk
We hold each other's hand
Walking together
No one judges us
Our hearts hug
Eyes happily smile
Voices oh… our voices
Souls molded
Birds… flowers… pink world…
No scars
Sun please some more time…
Don't wake me up
Not yet
Don't rise
Don't burn me sun

*

Ooh
No… our hands…
Injured smiles
Rainy eyes

It's not pink anymore
Yet
Another scar
Please let me stay
So, I can see him
And the birds will sing again
Let me stay there
Let the scars heal
Oh, no

*

We don't meet here
They said he is not here
Anymore
When will those scars heal?
Dead in real life
Sad soul
Burnt heart
Waiting for a dream
To get a life
In a dream
Our dream.

*****

The Call

I am waiting
Always waiting for that call
And you are not calling
You can make up my day
You can bring the light to my world
Simply you can make me happy
If you call
Why don't you call?
I don't blame you
I don't bleed you

I am not being demanding
And I never made you sad
But why don't you call?
Should I call?
As usual, should I?
Or I wait and wait and wait
Oh!
It's ringing, it's my call

Hello I missed you
I missed you too
I love you
I Lo…
Oh, I just woke up
It was a dream
Just a dream
Only
In my dreams
I can find you
You are a dream
And I will wait
Even if it's a dream
To be real
I will wait for that call
As usual
I will wait.

*****

Lost Heart

You were just a lost heart
With a different thinking
You put yourself in the shadow
Still, there is a light you brought out
And a love I brought in
I followed you blindly
You were such a character
Made me head over heels
Mesmerizing story
But

Our way was dividing; I couldn't catch up with you
And I let you down
Don't let go
And don't forget me

*

How could I leave you like that?
I missed you
Lost without you
I was selfish
No return back plan
And
I couldn't find you anymore
Dark absence
A scary big maze!
We lost the way and we are away

*

Being apart from you is sad
And
Being a part of you is a wish
I can't forgive myself
I am still searching for you
Maybe I was too crazy for you
But believe that I was too
Crazy about you.

*****

Sorry

Something went wrong
Often my fault
Right was wrong
River of tears
Yes, it was my fault

   I am 'sorry'… time took you from me and I surrendered…
                        thought it was right

Sadness was a punishment
Oh, I deserve it
Regret was too hard
Return was late
Young for pain

   I am 'sorry'… I wasn't happy… Leaving you was my
                biggest regret… imagine the pain

Songs were lies
Oscar in cheat
Reasons were faked
Rest was tortured
Years crawled fast

   I am 'sorry'… you waited for me and I didn't come back

Slap me
On my face
Retrieve your soul
Rage, I created
Yet, you felt

   I am so 'sorry'… I was selfish but I suffered … sorry is not enough for you and me.

*****

Magic

Before you go
Don't just leave
Cast a spell!
Let me forget
You and everything
Don't keep the tears
Don't leave the wounds behind
Let me forget
You and the memories
Don't say goodbye

Cast a spell
Let me forget
You with me
And if we meant to meet again
Don't charm me
Walk and just leave
And cast your magic
Chant it chant it
You don't know me
I don't know you
Cast your spell
Never meet again
Never meet again.

*****

MY Friend

Dear friend,
Since your absence
The past was nicer
Your memory was home
My laughter wilted

*

I still remember that day
Weird calls
Hesitant people talking
Questions no answers
Fear invaded my heart!
I asked
I searched
I dug
I found…
You're dead

I cried I cried I cried I cried I cried I cried
I cried I cried I cried I cried I cried I cried
I cried I cried I cried I cried I cried I cried

I drowned in tears

*

I saw you sleeping
You were beautiful
Beyond of me to
Say that goodbye
Oh
I stamp that kiss
On your forehead
And left with pain

*

Something was broken
The life was different
Dull without you
Sadness started
It was sad and sad

*

My friend!
Nothing can be said
It's just…
Your absence was too hard
Your absence ended the happiness
Your absence is still reminding me of you
And since you were gone
I just want to say
"Every day I miss you more than I miss you everyday"

****

"I miss you"
I didn't remember writing this, was it from her?

Up and Down

In my heart
Something was hidden
Real ghost
Forbidden area
Just for me and me
Mysterious like a puzzle
Enjoying not solving it
A secret!
Hush!

It's
Bouncing my heart
Up and down
And
Keeps it alive

The memories
Are heavy to carry
Drag me down to the bottom
And sometimes they
Fly me up to the moon
Up and down
Make me happy
And make me sad

Roller coaster rides
Drive me crazy
I laugh
I cry
Up and down
Up and down
I still hold tight
'And'
Head over heels!
I like it
Because…
My down fallings! Take me up to the top in love!

Just Tell Me

Tell me
Just tell me
How you are the way you are
The way you make me think about you
The way you make the way I am

Just tell me
Why I don't want to be just a number in your phone book
And why I want you to regret all my missed calls
Tell me why you are the salt of my life

And why I am ready to give you all the time of the world
when u ask for a second

Tell me
How you complete me
And how I am ready to gift my soul and heart to you
How this chemistry and biology and history between us
How my love to you is deeper than the oceans
And how I am over the moon when I am with you

Just tell me why you worth all my tears
And your smiles mean the world to me
Tell me why!
I want to occupy your thinking
And settle in your heart
Why I want to be
The first thing you think about when you wake up
And the last thing you see when your day is end
Who shaped you who impacted you?

Just tell me why I love you so much like so much
And how I love you the way I do love you.

*****

You are talking like Him

You are talking like him
You are acting like him
You are everything likes him
But,
You are not him
You are reminding me of him
I miss him
You are acting like him
You are laughing like him
You are joking like him
But you are not him
I want him

Why you are not him?
I miss him
I love him
Why … why… why
He hurt me
He cruelled me
He stabbed me
Will I love you one day?
Will you hurt me one day?
Will I have to leave you one day?
Don't be like him
He made me cry
He stabbed me many times
He broke my heart
I see him in you
He is almost you
I thought he's once in life
And no love likes his
Why did you appear?
You are nice…
Amazing… wonderful
He is not you
And you are not him
Then… Why?
I hurt you
I upset you
For revenge?
For satisfaction?
'No'
I should admit
'And'

Say the truth…
It's fear…
Fear to be hurt
Fear to be in love
Oh, Him!
NO!
BE different!
Change my past
Make a new memory
Happy one
New me and you
Just 'you' and 'me'.

******

Remember Me

We got separated
It was far a long time ago
Don't give up on me
Since I still remember you
You still remember me

*

I remember you as a tasty flavor
A taste I am addicted to
Like a favorite song playing on my head
Never bored with
Like a jumpy lovely beat in my heart
And I got used to
Our journey was
The first chapter of love
Overwhelmed me
And flourished my time
So, remember me
Because I love you

*

I will find my way back to you
Carrying all that love
Taking all the worries away
And unweight on our heavy hearts
You will get mad
Fight
Yell!
But you will accept
Because you love me

*

This journey needs a closure
And the memory is the anchor in our hearts
This should settle up our love

Don't let it sink
Just
Hold on
Remember me
I am coming back soon.
***

Cold Night

It's too cold tonight
Tears and rain
Thunder is crying
Darkness… everywhere
The night wears black
This night is sad
It's too crowded here
But I feel lonely
Too many voices
But I don't hear yours
I am calling you and you don't answer

I miss you, I am with you though
Too much pain
Too much tears
Tears are begging
Why don't you stay?
Many things I didn't say
Many answers you didn't hear
You are leaving… away
You are keeping the pain with me
Don't leave me alone
You don't answer
My eyes still begging
These tears seem endless

My heart is burning
Your hand is cold
My life started to be difficult
And peace, where I hope you rest.

*****

One Day

One day
We met
After all those years
Time altered you
And maybe me
But,
I knew you
You didn't
And that look

Eyes contact
If you gave it time
Your heart will tell you
That it's me
You just passed by
Leaving that broken one
With that cracked heart
You turned back!
You saw that tear
You saw it before
Many times
You were in my life
Chased me every where
Curse of the first love
Can't end it
I wiped that tear
Completed my way
Hurting me to let you behind
I wish I blinked when you appeared
We were never suitable for each other
And my heart will let go
One day.

*****

Red Flower

When I was a kid
There was a prince
Blonde with Blue eyes
I was running toward him and said: Good Morning
That was my prince
All used to say: "You are dreaming." 'You' are Dreaming!
And I was just a beautiful sweet hearted little girl
As all used to say

**

And I don't ask much
Like when my step sisters asked for
Jewels and gold
Perfumes and clothes
I asked for a red flower
My dad travelled and that red flower
Killed him down after meeting a beast
I was the beast beauty
As they called me!

**

I sank in sadness
I served my sisters
And angry step mother
I thought I deserved it
She was a witch
Never liked me
But I was liked by the birds and some tiny cuties
Relieving my sorrows
Remedy to my guilty heart
Joy in my sad life
One day there was a party
All the girls had to go
To meet a prince
Will he like someone with clothes covered in ash?
Am I Cinderella and is he, my prince?

**

But! Her mirror told her that I am the most beautiful girl ever
White like the snow
White hearted
Snow White
So, she had to stop me
Hide me

**

For the first time she was nice to me
She took me to the beach
And gave me that apple to taste!
Oh God!
I am transferring to something different
A girl with a fish tail
A lonely little mermaid
I was drowning more in my sadness

Deceived and thrown away
Salty tear… burnt heart

**

It was heavily raining that day
Dark ocean
Couldn't go up and meet the stars that night
Scary black clouds
But the
Thunder was calling me
To see that ship sinking
Someone drowns!
I hold him
I took him to the shore
The sun is rising
He opened his blue eyes and He is blonde!
He is my prince!
I said good morning!
Oh!
Someone is there approaching
With a royal procession!
I hid behind that big rock
She is holding my prince
She took him away
I want my prince back!

**

That witch
Knew the story

To give me my legs back
She will take my voice away till I gain his love
Within seven days
"*Seven days* you beautiful little mermaid
Others wise, you will be cursed with a dark black spell
Or you stab his heart!"

***

I have legs… I don't need to stab my prince, he will remember me
All this was meant to be
Oh, there he is…
The royal procession… the prince said:
"Good morning, did we meet before?"
Oh!
It's my good morning… But I can't answer
My voice is screaming inside me
Oh!

**

The castle and that lady!
She stole my Prince
The wedding is after seven days
Seven days
My prince it's me
My eyes plead you to feel me
But he said:
"Oh, your beautiful eyes… Why do I feel like we met before? What a pity you don't have a voice but, I am glad

that you will be the most beautiful guest in my wedding this week with the lady who saved me!"
Oh no… Remember me
But
You don't remember me
I can't stab you
Sad fate
Goodbye my prince

**

She is cursed and sleeping now
Numbed and alone
In a transparent glassy box

***

She didn't ask much!
Just a red flower
And she was just a Beautiful sweet hearted little girl
As all used to say!
But now
Her heart is dry and her pulse is sad
Sleeping beauty
Forever and for sure
Dreaming of her blue-eyed blonde prince

**

But the agony never last
Here her beautiful soul

Ascending to the destiny
Finding herself standing
In another world
Another beautiful world
Someone is calling?
"My Princess… My Princess"
He is calling her
"Am I dreaming?"
"No, you are not"
Smiled as he handed her
Her 'red' Flower.

*****

Inspired from immortal novels

- The beast and the beauty
- Cinderella
- Snow white
- The little mermaid
- Sleepy Beauty

One Sided

You are the one who I wish to see all the time
L. O. V. E.
The what, I feel towards you
And
YOU are there up high sky
I
Can't climb more
Can't feed that ego
My heart is exhausted
Listen to its beats
Spells love perfectly
Feel…

Sad heart with a Hopeless love
Falling apart
So, what do you think I feel when I am madly in love for you?
And you act as you don't know
I am
One-sided love.

Your beautiful smile
My eyes smiling back
Your smiles for others
My heart on pause
Waiting for a moment
Happy one
Thus,
Hurtful to my heart
And it's a contagious ache
My eyes have no right to tear
Hiding feelings… Dissolving my soul
Masking love… Devastating my all
Tornadoes messing me up
Tearing me apart
What do you think I feel when I shove my feelings away?
And you are acting blind
I am
One-sided pain.

When there is no sorrow
No agony and no suffering
Flourished hearts
Feelings are exposed
Love is everywhere
You giving me your heart
And, you listen to everything I say
Couldn't be happier
Nothing can overpower this love
What do you think I should feel when I make you a hero in my dreams?
And you are just a player in my fantasy
I am one-sided dream.

*****

What Did You Do

You beautiful
Sweetheart
Lovely… innocent
You pretty

Are you happy?
I am not
And I can't be more!

You gave me that feeling

A smile I draw when I see you
That sweet pain when we fight
A great pride when we make up
That tickles in my heart when I miss you
A love I've never felt before you
You took all this away
When you broke the bridges
And my soul was lost

What did you do?
'You' are a
Life cracker
Happiness stealer
Heart traitor
You are
Just a lie

Are you alive?
I am not and
And I can't be more
My heart is not clicking anymore
I don't feel that spark I used to feel
My heart had been injured and shredded by you
I can't forget you
I can't move on

What did you do to my heart!
Ur steps were fake and strategic
Made me angry and furious
I could barely keep myself together
What do you see when you look into a mirror?

How can you face yourself?
'Seek forgiveness'!
How can I heal?
When time didn't help!
You are fake and phony
But
Your stabs are too real and deep
Wise people don't believe lies
I wished I was *wise* that time and didn't believe you
You are a lie
Just a lie.

*****

She

What is she?
She is a devil
Just a devil
Plays hearts
Injures like a knife
A heart flourished with cruelty and drought
No sorrys no byes
Just vanishes
Like a mirage

As solid as rock
Damage digger

But, back then

She was
Innocent like an angel
Glowing like a flower
Smiling like a baby
Never guilty

As pure as pureness
Fairytales beauty

Why she gave up on herself?
What took that shine away?
Who created that dark devil inside?

Sometimes she lives in the past
Wishes to rewrite the time again
And find her heart
Where she kept it with someone
And lost them both

She is crying a lot and laughing a lot
You can see frozen tears … When you look at her eyes
She lost her heart
And she doesn't want it back
Maybe it is still there
Safe where she kept

She is proud and satisfied
Playing hearts
Injures them
Losing them
No sorrys no byes
Just vanishes
Like a mirage

She has a heart
For living
Not loving
She is very happy and satisfied
And just a devil
With a heart.

*****

They Said

You are a pain in my heart
A memory that squeezes it hard
You are the past which I still live in
They said, "the past is for visiting not for living"
And I say the past lives in us, marks and scars

*

This pain is painful
Guilty
As thorns run in my blood
Cut me off and I can't talk
They said, "the time can heal all the wounds"
And I say time can't heal the previous wounds, when it mixed with guilt

*

This silent secret
Between myself and I, gives me a tasteless life
Bitterness
Melting my heart
They said silence is the language of the great
And I say silence can kill you silently slow

*

I fake a smile and I laugh a lot
I am sad since I left you
I didn't know what I had until I lost it
Regret
And praying seeking forgiveness
They said, "regret things you didn't do"
And I say I do regret doing leaving you.

*****

What If

I am tired
Can't sleep
Exhausted
Fatigued
Drained
Pain
What a pain
That pain
Old pain
That IF!

*

What if I didn't miss that call that day?
And we talked for a long, long time
Would I keep you busy climbing up there
Or still that fall would take you away from us
And still, it would be the last time I hear your voice

*

She was sick
She liked me
When the visit was over
Something whispered to me to stay
I didn't
What if I stayed!
What if I spent some extra hours with her?
What if I listen to that call?
Would I have done something to save her?
Or still it would be the last time I see her

*

I thought I deserved a break
Punishing you
Revenge for the pain you caused
I took too long
And I punished myself instead!
What if I didn't overreact with that stubbornness?
What if I finished that parting early?
What if I just said that sorry?

Would I have not been strangled by that guilt?
Would I still be happy?
Or that parting was the fate

*

That if is painful
Hurtful
Devastating!
No one knows my pain
Stuck within a whirlpool
Always brings me back to the same beginning
Every night
Wake me up
Drown me down into that darkness
Makes me guilty and
Nothing can wash me up
Even my heavy tears on my poor pillow

*

That if is a game
Always takes me
To another level
Of sorrow
Endless game
Endless pain
That if
Old if.

*****

Good Bye

Goodbye dims the light of hope
Goodbye is the last word in love
Goodbye is the weapon of the weak
Goodbye is not a good-bye
It shouldn't be in any love dictionary
And never in our story
So, goodbye, goodbye.

This poem was supposed to be the last in this book but…

Piece of Sun
(My Horse)

A Piece of sun on the earth
Enlighten my ways
Erasing all the darkness
And the sadness
Piece of gold
Valuable
Priceless
His steps such music of life

Flourishing the soul
And. And his Neighing. Oh, what a symphony refreshing the whole world
Incredible
Beautiful warm lively
Like the wind
Oooo people he is a
Piece of sun on the earth
Really!
Really piece of sun
Blond… Beautiful
Bouquet of shines
Reflecting
Lights. Hopes…
And
Joy what a joy

And… and
'Why'! 'How'
I am falling apart
'Big' cloud
'Darkness'
Where is the light
Where is my joy
Who stole my happiness?
Who stole my treasure?
I am shaking, freezing
No warmth no lights
Sad Lost Cold
And my heart on fire
Fire what a 'fire'

Burning me apart

The sun had set
I buried my gold
And I wish if I could burry my heart with him

(2-9-2012 – 11-8-2021)
It was the best almost nine years with him…

*****

So?

What Is Sad

Am I sad or the life is sad?
Couldn't beat the shadows
They are everywhere
Once I catch a light
A big cloud steel it away
It's sad
The lights are there
Hiding from the shadows
I am sad and the life is sad
Never ending sadness

This pain is never gone and I can't carry it anymore
Is it my fate is to keep searching for lights?

'No'
I can't search any more
I won't search any more
Maybe
It will shine one day
Yes
One day
And
My special light
Will shine again too.

*****